Assassination Avoided,
Destiny Defined

Y. Rená Cooper

Marilyn

Thank you for always encouraging me in this walk into my destiny. Thank you for being supportive & making suggestions to push me further. May this book help you to help others.

Johnetta Rená Cooper

2-5-19

DEDICATION

Daddy God… This is actually Your book, I finally became the willing vessel. I give it back to You to do as You will. I would apologize for taking so long, but since You know all & You know me, You knew exactly how long it would take me to get this out. Thank You for loving me despite myself. I love You with all that I am.

To my FIRST best friend, my biggest cheerleader, my coach, and my mom, **Mary Ella Byrd-Cooper**. I miss you like crazy. You slipped out of the room before I could tell how much I needed you to stick around and not leave me. I know you are watching over me and cheering me on. All I ever wanted to do was to make you proud and I pray I have done just that. Thank you, Mary Ella for showing me true unconditional love, I love you forever, B.B.

To my dad, **Nemire Cooper, Jr**. I know I'm a late blooming "daddy's girl" because we both were too busy to spend much time. I know that many of the decisions that I have made in my life may have disappointed you, but I thank you for continuing to love me unconditionally, supporting me in my bad decisions and letting me learn my lessons the hard way. I believe in doing that, I am now stronger, and my past is just that…my past. Know that I love you and God couldn't have blessed me with a better father. The time together, jokes, funny conversations and slices of cake we share now are priceless. I think we've made up for lost time for sure. I love you, daddy.

To my FIRST true love & best friend, **Michael L. Banks, Sr**. Thank you for loving me unconditionally (30 yrs. is a long time). Ups, downs and in-betweens we always meet back in the middle. You helped me adjust to make it through the most difficult time in my life and showed me what true friendship is. It was a blessing to see you when I opened my eyes in my hospital room on 12/29/2008. You were my personal nurse and security all at the same

time. NO ONE got past you. You told me
that I would be okay and gave me your
strength to lean on. You also helped me to
see my value when I thought I had none.
Thank you for praying for me when I
couldn't pray for myself. Never could I
repay you for your labor of love. I'm so glad
that after all this time we will walk out the
rest of this journey together. You are my
forever and I thank God for you. You're
stuck with me for life whether you like it or
not (SMILE). I LOVE YOU.

To my besties, **Kenqwonna Moneak** &
Stephen Christopher Clarke. You all are a
package deal. I'm so glad that God allowed
us to cross paths and we decided to build a
lasting friendship from it. You both are
AWESOME people and GREAT pastors. I
am so blessed that I serve with you both in
ministry. And I'm even more honored that
you call me friend and invited me into your
family. Thank you for believing in me and
pushing me in ministry and the marketplace
when I needed it most. You guys ROCK

and I love you both. Thank you for blessing my book with the Foreword.

Ms. Faye Watkins… forever indebted to you. Your love and spiritual mentoring have helped me through the most turbulent times of my life. And being with my mom as she took her last breath… no words, you already know. My love for you is as far as your eye can see, actually farther.

To any woman or man who has been or is a victim of Domestic Violence. I pray that this book helps you to realize that there is always a way of escape. If you call out to the Lord for help, He will surely come. I understand that fear most times plays an intricate part of your staying, but if you Trust in God with all your heart and lean not to your own understanding, acknowledge Him in all your ways, He will surely direct your paths (make a way of escape). (Proverbs 3:5-6 paraphrased.) I dedicate this to you, because I too have been where you are now and by God's grace, I made it. YOU CAN MAKE IT TOO! Look to the hills for your help!

To the Survivor, continue to live life to the fullest in your after.

FOREWORD

It was a privilege for us to be asked to write the foreword for this amazing title – "Assassination Avoided, Destiny Defined." We have known the author for some time now, and that she is destined to do and produce great things in the earth. This book is significant because the fact that the author is alive to share the story is proof that God is real. When an individual is full of purpose and has a heart to fulfill that purpose, they are like a trick candle. The purpose flame in their heart and soul is difficult to extinguish. No matter what winds of life that blow in their in their direction, the resilient flame of destiny and determination burns hot.

This short read is more than just a story. This book is a resource for those who have been touched by abuse in any way. The author becomes transparent and vulnerable to expose the challenges, thought patterns and exit prayers of those who find themselves in an abusive relationship. Her explanations and perspectives are brief, but powerful enough to shatter the myths about what you thought you knew about victims and survivors of domestic abuse. Her words shift your thoughts about feeling stuck and hopeless, versus courageous and determined to live.

You will learn to identify cycles of abuse, to stop ignoring the signs and be reminded that despite challenge and hardship- your destiny is being defined. We all have a purpose to fulfill in life and sometimes it's just not always obvious to us during dark times. But whether you are a victim looking for the right moment to run for your life, a survivor working through recovery, or an angel assigned to assist; these pages will resonate with you.

May the oil of preservation, the favor, and destiny grace on both the message and the messenger of this book be your portion. We whisper a short and powerful prayer that God's protection and perfect will be done in the lives of every reader. May His Word be a lamp to your feet as you escape every literal and spiritual assassination of the enemy and your destiny be defined.

Sincerely,

#TeamClarke

ACKNOWLEDGEMENTS

My Sister **Stacia**, nephews and nieces, **Marquis & Drake, Shonna and Sydnye** & my other mom **Margie**, I LOVE YOU ALL!

Evelyn Pullum thank you for risking your life. **Jonathan & Cameron** 'Te-te' loves you.

Debbie Pearson… **Allan & Modise Shipman, Sr**…. you all know (more like sisters and brother instead of cousins). I Love you.

My daughter **Ashley Banks**. Thank you for allowing me in your and Ziyah's heart. Hugs and kisses.

The **Byrd** and **Cooper Families** and ALL of my extended family (far too many to name)… Thank you, Thank You, Thank You. My love to you all.

My extended family:
God-parents **Wayne & Doris Brady**, the **Murrays**, the **Washingtons**, the **Tates**, the **Gordons**, the **Perrys**, & the **Blands**, you all have been a huge support. More than you know.

Ciara & Brit Watkins… you both played a significant part during that time. Not sure if I ever told you how, but know I got you.

Rolanda L. Brady you're not here physically, but I know you would still be on me about writing this book. Thank you for the journals that got me to this point. Your seed sown is coming to harvest. I miss you, sis.

So many others I could or should acknowledge by name… please charge my head not my heart and the fact there is not enough pages in this book.

IN MEMORY OF

Fertamia 'Tammy' Smith, your death at the hands of someone else, was not in vain. Though we don't understand why God chose to give you your mansion early, I know that Heaven is a whole lot funnier because of it. You are forever in my heart… And I thank God I got the opportunity to tell you! It's because of you that I have the strength to write this book. Psalm 27:1-5

Trinity Ann Banks, we were just beginning to build this wonderful thing called a relationship. Thank you for blessing your dad and I before your leaving us. Thank you for adding to me and my life with your presence and your smile. Thank you for calling me 'mom'.

Table of Contents

INTRODUCTION 18

WHO AM I? 23

YOU'VE GOT TO BE HONEST 38

MY NORMAL 43

DECEMBER 28th 54

MY FAITH MADE STRONG 66

THE CYCLE OF ABUSE 69

AN UNSPECIFIC PRAYER 72

GOD CARED FOR ME 77

WHEN THEY ARE READY TO TALK 83

THERE IS A WAY OUT 87

WE ALL SEE THE SIGNS 95

I CAN'T SEE MY REFLECTION 111

DESTINY DEFINED 116

INTRODUCTION

Where do I begin? I have tried several times in the last 10 years to write this book. My emotions always seemed to get the best of me. So, still in my emotions, I have made a conscious decision to press through and tell some of my story. With the prayer that if it helps just one person, I have done what God has wanted me to do. So many people have heard my testimony and have said, 'There is a book in you.', 'Rená, you have to tell your story.', or 'So many women and/or men need to hear this and will be delivered by your book'. I fought within my mind on many a day or maybe it was the enemy, adversary, devil (whatever you call the thing that holds you back), about writing this book. I began to feel that my story or testimony doesn't hold the 'weight' that it held when it happened 10 years ago. I feel that my story is just like so many other stories out there, so why wouldn't my test be any different from the next person? I finally decided to ask God, most times I don't ask for fear of His answer. He answered me one day when I took the time to sit quietly and wait for an answer or answers (that would preach, laugh out loud). First, He told me that this really wasn't about me. Yes, it happened to me, but it has nothing to do with my past or the things I may or may not have done wrong. See God is not a God that punishes us like people think He could or would. He truly is a loving and forgiving God that wants the best for us, those He created in His image. So, nothing I did wrong in my past cause my traumatic incident. Second, why not me? God allowed many things to happen to those who He cherished or chose in the bible. They went through tests and trials. I don't mirror myself to Job or Jesus, but if God chose them to go through and they came out alright, then WHY NOT Rená? And reason number three; He gave me the grace to come out victorious no matter how bad it looked to me as I was going through it. I recently asked myself (as I have many times), why now? Why am I ready to tell the story now? Why not when I got home from the hospital? Why not five years ago? Why do I feel in year 10 that I am "ready"? Well, I took the time to do a little research on the number 10. Numbers are a part of our everyday life. Spiritually, numbers have great significance, so I decided to look up the number 10. Ten is considered a perfect number at least in urban society. Example: she is a 10 meaning she is perfect on a scale from one to 10. I also found out that 10 is the completed course of time or completeness in divine order. If I believe that EVERYTHING happens for a reason and things must come to past in DUE SEASON then, this is the SET time and season 10 years later, that this book is now ready to be written, shared and received by the world. I cannot lie; fear, disappointment, depression, suicidal thoughts, anger and bitterness have played a large part in my life these past years. But with prayer, love from my family & close friends and time I believe that I have pressed past these emotions. NOW I believe it is time for Assassination Avoided, Destiny Defined. My prayer is that this book blesses you, as I walk this out... tears and all.

With love for God's people,

Y. Rená Cooper

WHO AM I?

Hello, I'm Rená... have we met? I laugh to myself every time I say that. Why, well most times it's to my friends who know me but may have forgotten who I am so to speak. Let me give you an example. I can be very sarcastic at times (I get it from my dad), so when I say or do something my friends think I shouldn't have done or said, I just re-introduce myself. But for you the reader, I want to tell you a little bit about me, so let me introduce myself. My name is Yolunda Rená Cooper, founder and CEO of 4 My Voice Matters. A 501(c)3 organization that advocates for and brings awareness about domestic violence & suicide. I work for the government and I am living my best life now.

Not a perfect life, but better than years past. There was a time that I didn't think that I would be alive, let alone writing this book and talking to you. When people ask me to describe myself, I would always shy away from it because there was a time that I didn't like me. I didn't like the way I looked (still sometimes an issue), I didn't like my job, I didn't like the direction that my life was going, I didn't like my mate, I just didn't like anything.

Fast forward to now, we can revisit some of those places a little later. I am a person who now believes in affirming yourself. Words are very powerful so before I get into the meat of this book, I am going to give you a few words that describe who I am after I began to learn to like and even love myself.

Daring… I am a thrill seeker now. After going through all that I have, I enjoy a good roller-coaster ride from time to time. Well actually as often as I can. I am a season pass holder to our local amusement park and will sometimes go to the park two or three times in one week. I also once jumped from a perfectly good airplane, on purpose. Gasp, imagine that. I laugh all the time at that. People use planes to get from one destination to another and I decided that I prefer to jump out of one, with a parachute of course but jumped from the plane is what I did. I loved every exhilarating, nervous moment of the entire experience.

Resilient… recently I had the opportunity to participate in a calendar and I had to choose a word that described me in my winning moments. I choose resilient because it took me a while, but I realize that I have 'bounce back'. For me to survive the events that lead to the book you hold in your hands I had to overcome some things that most people could not. I know that it was with the help and grace of God that I made it, and for that reason I know that if I made it through those things, I can make it through anything. And the blessing is that I recovered quickly.

Amazing… this is more so a word about how I feel rather than me being. After years of battling depression and low self-esteem, I have to say, majority of my days I feel absolutely amazing. I keep reminding myself that life could be so different if things had made a turn in a different direction. I wake up most days feeling more positive about the direction my life is going in now, then it was 10 plus years ago. Things are bright where they were once dim or even dark. I as the song says, can see clearly now.

Now that I have briefly gave you a little bit about me, let's get into this book, shall we?

Miracles happen. Humph, God does have a bigger plan. Sometimes life feels so extra, that it doesn't seem like there is a purpose. It definitely doesn't feel like there is a destiny in sight. You feel like all you can do is push to barely get through the day. The same routine every day. The alarm goes off, breakfast needs to be fixed, you're going to sit in some traffic just thinking… it's going to be a while before the day is over. So many of us live our lives on the edge of losing. Feeling like there is no win in site. We're unaware of what our life is leading us to, some of us are just unwilling to see it. Worse yet, sometimes rather than living the magnificent life that God had planned for us, our life is a living hell. Humph, a hell of our own choosing. It feels like there is no escape. Feels like there is no way out. Stuck in the same relationships, stuck in the same jobs, it's the same every single day. Well listen, I'm here as a survivor today to tell you that there is a way out. There is nothing that God hasn't already provided, there is no way of escape that He hasn't produced for you. There is no situation you're in, no circumstance, there is no relationship. I'm going to share my story with you. I'm going to talk to you about how I got out. And trust me, before it happened, I couldn't see it coming. But how amazing, is it that we serve a God that always makes a way of escape, I Corinthians 10:13. If it feels impossible to you, I want you to know that it's right here for you. It's those moments in life, when we feel like there is no out, when we feel like there is no solution to the problems that we are having, there are no answers to the questions that we have. It's a sure sign that you're right there, breakthrough is just around the corner. You can move from the edge of death, to living in destiny. Believe me when I say this, and I am telling you this at the very beginning for a good reason. You can see your purpose fulfilled, and you definitely can see destiny defined. Moving away from the edge of death and living in destiny is something that will seem possible when you're done with these pages.

It doesn't seem real. My life today is so far removed from where it was. Now I'm going to tell you some things in this book and share some pretty private things. Right now I'm just talking about every day stuff. To look at my life now, I never would have imagined. Well let me be honest, some stuff we do imagine, but it's just that... in your imagination. You're not thinking that this stuff is really going to happen. There is always a maybe, or a could be, or might be, but my life today is so far removed from where it was. There are times that I can't even believe how much I was hiding. Now that I am standing in the front, traveling throughout the country, speaking in front of rooms of people, on live videos, the 'world wide web', stop it, ha. I've been on the radio, I have been on podcasts. I look back at my life and all I can do is be grateful and thankful for all that I have. See, sometimes it's very easy to get spoiled to the things that you are used to, the way that you're accustomed to living. It easy to just take things for granted. But right now all I can do is be grateful. I'm thankful, and if you know me you will hear me say this a lot. I thank God for my good government job. I thank God for the 501(c)3 non-profit that

I've started, just a few short years ago that's a complete success called, 4 MY VOICE MATTERS, NFP. This organization is amazing, because it helps people know truly that their voice carries weight. I love being a person that people can confide in. To know something about me is to know that I care about people. That I listen to them. Now sometimes I do interrupt while they are talking, because I get excited. I'm so excited and so passionate about the things that they're saying that I need them to hear what I am saying about what they are saying. I love the fact that domestic violence victims can come and share their deepest secrets in confidence but walk away with a plan. I also love being the person that can provide safe spaces for people to share without being fearful. Fearful of what? Fearful of being judged. Fearful of what? Fearful of their business being all over the street. They can share without fear – safe space. If you know anyone going through something and you're their listening ear, remember that they are trusting you. Remember that they are depending on you. Remember, safe space. You know, there are several people that have to come and confide in me and tell me their stories, but they weren't ready to release them yet. They didn't, feel comfortable yet. But even though they were or are still on that side of abuse and being on that side of abuse can be tricky, they needed someone to talk to. I'm loyal to a fault. Accommodating, I am everybody's friend, even though everybody is not my friend, I still show up for people. I'm still the consistent one. I'm still the one who will drive across town even when no one will come pick me up. Have you ever been in relationships like that? Yeah, I see you nodding your head, I hear you snickering to yourself. Because you know exactly what I am talking about, being loyal to a fault. But let me tell you something you don't know about me that I briefly mentioned before, I'm also daring. I live life to the fullest now, not because I almost lost my life, I will tell you about that in a little while. I'm not afraid to try things, I've been like that since I was young. Ha ha ha, remember I told you, I'm the one who will ride all the roller coasters, and I'm the one who will jump out of perfectly good airplane. I'm the one who will go to another state just to sit in a seat that will pull me down into the ground and throw me 600 ft into the air. I did it five times in a row, I even have video. My friends put me on live when this happened, they just couldn't believe it. I just kept going back it was so exhilarating. At one point sitting on the Sling Shot no one wanted to ride with me any more so they had to put a bucket in the seat next to me, because that's how daring I am. But sometimes when challenges hit our lives even the most daring person shrinks. Even the most daring person becomes silent. There is no more laughter, no more screaming or excitement. Just silence and sadness. I'm so excited that I can live life to the fullest now, because I did almost lose my life. So I'm not afraid anymore. I'm open to new adventures. I'm also very simple. Now you may say, how can you be daring and simple at the same time? Well I am. Because I don't like a lot of fuss about a lot of things. I'm down to earth. Just a common girl with big dreams, big aspirations, but I can also be complex as most of you. I am proud that at almost 48 years old (even though I don't look it, ha... girlish looks sticking around, gotta love it) I'm successful, and most importantly, I'm trusted. The excitement fills me with joy. I'm so excited that you're with me to take this ride, to hear this story, because it's going to shift you. Maybe you've been through what I've been through. Maybe you know someone who has. Or maybe you're the offender. However you look at it, I know that sharing the words that are on these pages is going to change some lives, saves some lives, and help some people know that their voice truly does matter.

YOU'VE GOT TO BE HONEST

If I had to describe my life in a nutshell, I would say that I've lived a complicated and complex life. But, the one thing I know is that I have a destiny. What is destiny? Destiny is the events that will necessarily happen to a particular person or thing in the future. That means that for years I've know that certain things in my life were happening and setting me up for this very season of my life. Deep down I knew that if I survived the heartache, disappointment, embarrassment, and brief phase of denial - that I was going to fulfill a higher purpose in life. At one point in time, I didn't think I would ever be free of my situation. I felt like even though I had all these grand plans and aspirations, I was stuck! There was no way out for me. I've always been somebody who is overly friendly and very outgoing. So, when I meet people I have this knack for connecting and making people feel like we've known one another for a long time. This is a gift, but curse at the same time. In today's society, my "connecting gift" has made me what I would call "Facebook famous". A lot of people on Facebook like my page, they've seen me, liked my posts, and commented on pictures. But, the question is do they actually know me? A lot of them can't say that they know the real me, only what I show and share on my social media platforms. They know that version of Rená. However, even in the social media version of myself, I do my very best to be real and authentic. I'm that shot of tequila with no chaser. I shoot from the hip and I don't sugar coat anything. So, one thing that people always can get from me is the naked and raw truth. I'm not going to try and make something look better than what it actually is. I don't look at the world through rose colored lenses. I like to convey the vivid Technicolor perspective that I see life happening from. I look at situations and people for what they are, and try to avoid assuming anything else. Why am I making a big deal about being authentic right now? Because, sometimes when we distort our images or our views, that's when we get messed up. I just want you to understand that even though you may be going through something, or you are in the midst of something that may be traumatic and devastating, part of coming out on the other side is being honest. On our jobs, in school, marketplace or ministry, we don't share every detail of ourselves. In most cases we can't because it's not always appropriate. As I stated before though, if you fail to see and acknowledge things for what they really are, you will get off track. You have to call it like it is to avoid denial and delay. Challenge and hardship is designed to smother the very life out of us. But, you are divinely designed to beat the odds, survive, and succeed. Where you think that there is no hope, or you think that you may not come out of it - I want to be that one glimmer of light through the pages of this book to show you that you can and will come out of it. There is life after whatever you've been through, and you can live your best life after. This chapter is all about stressing the importance of being honest, first with yourself and regarding the situation you are facing right now. How do I know that you can come through it and live your best life after? Keep reading and allow me to share my experience with you.

MY NORMAL

As of this year, October 26, I am a ten-year domestic abuse survivor. I was in an abusive relationship for over 15 years. I was married to my abuser on paper for ten, but I was thrown out of our home four days before our 9th year wedding anniversary. What I tell people all the time is that I likened my story to the script of a Lifetime story. Not a burning bed story - and that's telling my age, if anybody remembers the old Farrah Fawcett movie, Burning Bed. It wasn't an everyday physically abusive situation. Although it could be almost every day for emotional, verbal or mental abuse because sometimes just an evil look, a wrong word or silence can be a form of abuse. So for me, living in that environment, became my normal even though I didn't like it. I thought of several ways to get out of it, many different times. Thinking about an exit, dreaming of life outside this normal was one thing. Making my exit included these considerations: I took a vow for "better or worse", I truly loved my spouse and wanted to fight for happiness together, and some days I feared the consequence of an escape attempt going wrong. See most people think that "leaving" is just about you. They fail to consider the safety of all those connected to you. It's not unheard of for an abuser to target family, friends, co-workers, and sometimes complete strangers when they are upset with you. So, you stay silent, frozen, and fearful, so not to make a wrong or risky move.

Sometimes, on the days that things would get physical, it would take me on an express ride into a deep depression. Such a rough, bumpy ride that I wouldn't go to work for a few days. Mental health is real and debilitating. When your mind and soul are aching everything stands still. It's as if time stops for hours, days, and even weeks at a time. Any type of abuse can ruin your entire life by domino effect alone. Me taking days off would cause more abuse. Because now it's verbal reprimands, like "Why are you at home? You need to be at work! You need to make my money!" Or, if I was battered so much that I had bruising, of course I would do all I could to try to cover it up with makeup and there was never enough to hide the bruises. I would try not to go to work, because I didn't want to be talked about or for my coworkers to guess or assume what I was going through. I really didn't want to have to make up a lie about how I got the bruises, or why I'm extra quiet today, and not socializing. Some of the darkest days would be days when we would get into a huge argument or disagreement and then he would disappear for two or three days at a time. I didn't know what to expect when he would return. Would he be in a calm state, or would he be more enraged then what he was when he left?

I remember one of the worst moments where I compromised myself. Just being very transparent, my ex-husband was a habitual cheater as well as an abuser. Even though I'm a woman of faith and had asked God many times to change things. When a woman gets tired of things going a certain way and we get fed up; sometimes we do things without thinking or we over think. I felt if God wasn't listening or He wasn't moving as fast as I thought He should, since I was asking for God to fix it, to fix him. I had gotten to a point where I felt like, "Well, if he is cheating--," not saying two wrongs make a right but, "If you are going to do what you are going to do and without any consideration of me. Then I'm going to do what I'm going to do. You keep doing you, and I'm going to do me." I remember having a conversation one evening after confronting him about the "girlfriend" he had for several years during our marriage. I asked him was he going to stop the relationship and be my husband. He of course denied any indiscretions and told me that if he was cheating, I deserved it. I then told him I was done with our marriage. He laughed of course and told me that it wasn't over until he said the marriage was over. I remember being very stern and I told him our marriage was over, and I found a friend, since he had been unfaithful our entire marriage. How did I know this? Let's just say my sister gave me the nickname 'Inspector Gadget' after the cartoon character. If my antennas went up or my gut instincts kicked in I was going to find out by any means necessary. I guess he didn't believe me. One evening approximately a month after the previous mentioned conversation he asked where I had been after I was gone all evening. Because I was tired and had told him my intentions previously, I told him I was out with my friend like he had been out with his. Enraged he pushed me into our car and drove to a parking lot in proximity and beat my face so badly, it was disfigured on one side. After that beating, he held a gun to my head and played Russian roulette. Which was almost one of the most terrifying things I had to experience... almost.

That night he wanted to take me to the emergency, but I refused to go. I should have taken pictures, but I never did. He forced me to go the next afternoon when the swelling wouldn't go down. Now mind you, I've never called the police during our entire relationship. Imagine my embarrassment when the police came to talk to me. I couldn't talk to tell the truth so my husband told them I was assaulted by some women, because I was messing around with one of the lady's guy. I wish they could have saw the fear in my eyes and know that my nod in agreement with his story was a lie. One of my good friend's husband was working in the emergency room that evening and saw us in the room, we were there for what seemed like an eternity. The look on his face let me know that I had to look horrible. I was so afraid of what he would say. What he would think. Did he know? My husband again did the talking and gave a different lie. I knew that I could expect a call from my friend in the hours to follow and I didn't know what I would say. Guess I was relieved that I couldn't talk. Maybe she would forget or figure I would need rest once her husband told her what I looked like. When I close my eyes and I think back to that time, looking in the mirror at myself, it reminded me of the elephant man on the left side of my face. The swelling didn't go down for three or four days. So, of course I took off work again. When the swelling finally went down, I had to deal with the black eye that was still left behind. If he would have kept hitting me on the left side of my face, it probably would have shattered my jaw bone, but he did not. This had become my private normal. Even after this incident I stayed another two years. I mention this because I want those of you who are in similar situations or have survived similar situation to know that if you think no one understands your struggle, I do. If no one understands why you stay longer than someone else says you should, I do. But as I mentioned before I am a praying woman. I prayed and prayed and prayed some more. I remember praying in July two years AFTER the beating, AFTER he vowed never to put his hands on me in a harmful manner again, AFTER purchasing us a three bedroom, one and a half bath, split level home for us, I prayed asking God for an exodus. Begging and pleading with God to get me out of this normal I had vowed to live in for so long. Then it happened. One very cold October, October 26th to be exact, it was the last fight/argument we would have. No coat, no keys, no phone, he threw me out of our home, my home. I'm going to fast forward past all the details for now, but God had answered my prayers. How? I was "out" and still alive. This was a miracle, but nerve wrecking at the same time, because, I didn't know what to expect next. Was he just going to finally leave me alone and let me go? I didn't know for sure. What I did know is that I had a very short period of time to decide what to do next. I had to be careful and make calculating decisions to keep me and those I loved safe. Deep in my heart though, I was waiting for the other shoe to drop. Remember when I said the beating in the parking lot was "almost" the most terrifying experience of my life.

DECEMBER 28th

On December 28th, I was coming home from a church service. A pastor who I was acquainted with, she later became and still is my best friend, invited me to the last church service of the year that they were having in their location before they moved. At first, I wasn't going to go, but I decided to go at the last minute. I sat in the service uninterested. Not moved and surely not wanting to be social. I knew most if not all the members of the church so they were trying to get to me when service was over. I just wanted to go, so I tried to leave quickly. As I was exiting the church, she instructed everyone to stop. It was after dismissal, and she said, "I need to pray. I've got a strong sense of premature death. Not that I believe somebody is going to die, but death is going to come very, very near. I don't know if it's anybody in my family or if it's somebody in your family or if it's someone here in the church, but I think we need to pray." So she prayed against the spirit of premature death. She prayed, and I remember her praying hard. I was there physically, but mentally I checked out before I arrived. She probably prayed for a good 10 or 15 minutes, I don't even remember what she prayed exactly, I just stood there with my hands lifted in obedience, but ready to go. She closed the prayer, told us she loved us all and then I left without talking to anyone. The church was on the south side of Chicago and I was driving back to the western suburbs, which is probably about a 35-minute drive. While driving I was just contemplating my next moves. I had just filed for divorce on December 8th and I was thinking, "How do I start over? Being with someone over 15 years, how do I begin life again? I'm about to be single again, how do I do this? How or where do I start?" Even though he was my husband, 150 plus people celebrate us on our wedding day nine years before, we pretty much lived like roommates, everything was split down the middle, so to me it was more like an arrangement instead of a marriage. But how do I pay bills fully on my own? I've never really lived on my own before. I went from my parent's house, to school, back to my parent's house, to being married. So how do I learn how to be on my own, independent of my parents? The ride home became kind of short, because I had all this stuff going on in my mind. It was three days from the New Year, I didn't really have any plans, but I knew I needed to plan something. I pulled into my parent's driveway. Their driveway is on the side of the house, it was a bungalow style home. If you are facing the house, the driveway is on the right side of the house. I got out of my car. I only had my truck keys, a pocket Bible and that was it, because I keep my identification and valuables somewhere on my person and I don't carry a purse. I was walking towards the porch of the house and I saw a guy come from behind the tree in front of the house who was on a cellphone. I thought he was headed for the neighbor's house because someone there would have frequent visitors. It was dark outside and cold. It was probably between 10:15 and 10:20 at night. The streetlights and glow from a light in front of the house barely allowed me to see the guy, but I knew it wasn't anybody I recognized. At first he was walking toward the neighbor's house, but then he began to walk at an angle toward me.

Inside the house was my mom, my dad, my sister and my two nephews. I remember him putting the phone in his pocket and when I was almost to the porch, I thought, "Well I don't know him, and he hasn't said anything yet. He hasn't said, "Excuse me," or "Could you help me?" or anything, so I thought I could be in trouble, but I wasn't sure. I did not want to take him to the door of the house, because I had no way of alerting the people inside that there was somebody unknown outside of the house beside me. I was afraid that if he was going to rob or assault me, that he could possibly force himself in and everybody inside could be hurt or killed and it would be my fault. I decided to turn back around to go back to my truck and I thought, "I'm going to get inside my truck and I'm either going to call the police immediately and he's going to go away or I'm going to run him over with my truck if he tries to do anything to the vehicle or to me." I got halfway to the vehicle and he called me an explicit name and told me not to move. So when I turned and looked at him, I saw that he had pulled a pistol out of his pocket. I stood there, and realized, I didn't have anything but my truck keys in my hand. All I saw was two of the coldest eyes I had ever seen, next to my ex-husband's eyes the last time he had jumped on me. Even though there was no light outside, I could still see from the glow of the streetlight that he just had no emotion whatsoever in his eyes.

He cocked the pistol.

I couldn't believe it. I'm not moving. I'm not giving you any resistance or anything, so why would you even cock it? My first thought was to run. I turned to my right to run towards the porch, and that's when the first shot went off. I believe now after knowing everything that happened, that that shot was the one that put a hole the size of a quarter in my 12th vertebrae and nicked my spinal cord. I remember hitting the ground and I didn't have feeling in my legs. He stood over me and shot me three more times and then just walked away into the darkness.

I don't know if it was a blessing but never lost consciousness. I was able to yell out and scream for my life. I learned later that several neighbors heard me and several calls to 9-1-1 were made within minutes of one another. My next-door neighbor came out on her porch calling my name, asking where I was. I told her I was in the grass, and she told me to hold on, and that she had 9-1-1 on the phone. My sister did not hear me screaming, although she and my nephews were in the living room. What I found out that night for sure is that the love of a mother is powerful. Why? My mother, who was in the back of the house, in the kitchen to be exact, heard me cry out and sent my sister out to find me. She found me in the grass, and she came, and she held me. By that time though, I had pretty much made peace with God, there was such a calm that came over me. I didn't think that I was going to make it. In my limited mind as - much as I believe in God, I knew God was and is a God of miracles - my mind was limited to thinking that death was for me. So, I made peace with Him, God that is. I asked God for forgiveness of all my transgressions and I told my sister, "I'm okay. If I go, I'm okay." She prayed, and she told me I wasn't going to die and that I was going live. She held me a kept repeating that I shall live and not die until the ambulance and police arrived.

The police finally came. It seemed like forever, but they were probably there within five minutes or less of the first call made by neighbors. I was taken by ambulance to the hospital. I never lost consciousness until they put me under for surgery. I even kept my sense of humor and made sarcastic threats to the ambulance driver who hit every single pothole on the way to the hospital. I found out that I was in surgery for four and half hours. When I came to, at what I know was the next afternoon or evening, I realized that I didn't have feeling in my legs. I couldn't move, the nurses and my family were instructed that I had to lay perfectly still and flat on my back. Here is where the blessing come from this almost tragedy. I learned I was shot four times. One bullet was an "in and out", one bullet grazed the center of my back, two bullets ricocheted off of every organ in my body, except for my heart, as I stated before it put a hole in my vertebrae and nicked my spinal cord, and my lungs collapsed on the operating table, causing them not to be able to remove those two bullets. It seemed very grim.

The shooting wasn't going to take me away though.

I got feeling in my legs after two and half days. I was up walking by the fifth day, out of the hospital by the eighth day. And within nine months of the shooting the bullets that were once under my lungs traveled to the right side of my body where they were removed by surgery. I tell people then and now that if they didn't believe in miracles before, they are look at one every time they look at me.

I must give my disclaimer with this life event: Fact - I did see my assailant and it wasn't my ex-husband.

MY FAITH MADE STRONG

Some would have given up, some would have felt defeated, some may have laid in that hospital bed and pronounced their own death. But I will tell you one thing, this trauma strengthened my faith in God. I grew up in church and went faithfully with my mom but didn't encounter God until my 20's. I had seen so many people go through so many different things, and my life wasn't perfect, but I just never really thought that some of the things that happened to me, would happen to me. I was always that one to never say never, but I still never thought that I would fall "victim". So what did I get out of it? People may read my story and think the same thing I thought at one point in time. I thought that God was letting me down. I thought that he had forgotten me, and that the destiny I dreamed of would never be fulfilled or defined. What I learned out of this life lesson is that God gives us all free will and choices to make. Even though He may guide us, send us signs and signals, we have our own decisions to make. We may pray for guidance and change, but He still gives us freewill. I say the same about my ex-husband. I begged God to work on my marriage, and sometimes I saw change that looked like we were going in a new direction. While in the end God released me and told me that it was okay to not feel responsible for my marriage failing. It's was if Holy Spirit would nudge me on the shoulders during private moments when I would cry asking God why my world was falling apart and the small still voice would whisper, "Don't feel discouraged about the rejection that you feel. Don't blame yourself for not feeling the love that you are longing for and are missing". God ministered to me that my husband could not give what he didn't have available, because of his own needs, and selfish choices. The husband I thought I had, was trapped behind anger, hurt, rejection, depression and his own insecurities. At that time in our lives and marriage, my love couldn't reach him and neither could the agape love of Christ. So, I had a choice of my own to make. It was time for me to choose. I chose me.

THE CYCLE OF ABUSE

It was a cycle, and when it comes to the abusive cycle, some days he'd love me, and he would show me love repeatedly and tell me that he'll never do it again. Other days, the rage would build back up, where he's agitated about something or someone (possibly me or not) and then the abuse would happen again. Therapist share the circular model of abuse in counseling, like educators and professors share it in class when they are teaching about abuse. There is a honeymoon period, and then there is a calm phase. After the calm phase tension builds, and the final phase is another abusive incident. I'd like to reference a free graphic provided by the

TherepistAid.com that helps you visualize the cycle. The thing about abusive cycles is that they must be broken, before a life is lost. Like the circle that forms a wedding band, symbolizing the covenant that is not meant to be broken. The same circular cycle of abuse can symbolically wrap around your mind, heart, and neck, to smother the life from you if you don't choose to boldly break it in your life. Trust me, I know better than most that this is easier said than done. But, desperate times, almost always call for desperate measures. While in my cycle of abuse God told me that He gave my ex-husband freewill. He tried to move him, and God is a gentleman, so he tried to guide his heart and show him right from wrong, let him know that I was a gift to him. And, my ex-husband still chose to be abusive. He still chose to make excuses, he chose not to get help. He also still chose to be with other women, instead of me. He chose not to take care of and honor the gift that God gave him. Even in spite of all of that, in the end because I am here now, because I have a story to tell and God cared enough about me to make me a testimony, just like he has done to many other people that have endured this pain. God chose to make me a light, a glimmer of hope to show somebody that life can be better on this side of abuse. You just have to make a conscious decision. You must decide to break the cycle. No one can make the decision for you.

AN UNSPECIFIC PRAYER

I was shot and I almost lost my life, and as I mentioned before, I prayed hard for exodus in July of 2008. Looking back, what I failed to do is be more specific with my prayer. I just told God that I wanted out of this marriage. My exodus came when I got thrown out of my house on October 26th (two month and two days before I was gunned down). So, even though it seemed cruel, I got what I asked for, I just wasn't specific in saying, "Well God, I want an exodus, but I want to be safe." Or, "God, I want an exodus, but I want to be able to keep my government job that's going to help me take care of myself. God, I want to have my own place, so

I don't have to be dependent on my parents or anybody else. Or, "God, I want there to be peace and for us to be able to split amicably and be okay." I wasn't very specific. So I've learned in prayer to be more specific. I've learned that on this side of abuse, that God always loved me, still loves me and wants the best for me. I learned to listen to myself, whereas I didn't listen to myself before. I didn't trust my gut and I didn't believe in myself enough to stand flat footed or leave earlier in the relationship when I had an opportunity to, for fear of not wanting to be alone or afraid of being called a failure and fear of him. Or not enter the relationship at all when I saw the first red flag.

You see the abuse that I had endured, and the eventual attempted assassination had been horrendous, but God had a bigger plan. He had taken this person that I was, and He instilled a strength that I never knew was possible for me to have. My life wasn't perfect, and most of the time I had not walked with God as I could or should have. I remember even at one point, I thought God was letting me down, and I was disappointed because I saw Him doing for others and not me. I had to realize that God gives us all freewill. We are the ones to make choices that can help us, hinder us or hurt us.

I had to realize, as I began to heal, both physically and spiritually, that God had actually given me what I had asked for, I just didn't realize it. Let me explain. I had begged God to help my marriage, and He did. I wasn't specific. My exodus was my help. God loves me so that He wanted the best for me and since God wouldn't abuse me why would He allow anyone else to abuse me. One day in the abusive cycle, things would be good, and then my now my ex-husband would get agitated, then he would calm down and tell me that it would never happen again. Then he began to tell me all the reasons that it was my fault that he had hit me or yelled at me or hurt me in some way. "Look what I had made him do", would always be my ex's answer. I heard God's voice tell me one day, that He had tried to woo my husband back to Him and our marriage, but at the end of the day, my ex had freewill too and he had chosen to be abusive and unfaithful. Each of us have our choices in life.

GOD CARED FOR ME

I choose right now to take my story, to tell you about how much God cared for me, and how God has made me a testimony. He allowed me to live so that I can tell you that life can be better on the other side of abuse and divorce. You see, it has to do with how we ask God for things. I had prayed so many times, "God give me an exodus out of this." And I had gotten what I asked for. I was thrown out of my house and shot with the intent to kill me, but it was because I hadn't been specific. I had learned that if we need to pray, to be more specific. God always loves me. He always wants what's best for us. But I needed to learn that I had also had to trust myself. To listen to myself. And when I heard that voice in my gut that told me something was wrong, I needed to believe it and to trust in it. Just like God cared for me. Loved me, and provided a way of escape. He will do it for you, and He cares for you just like He cares for me. He has no respect of persons (Romans 2:11). What he will do for one he will do for another. No matter what your negative self-talk and insecurities are telling you right now, you have destiny inside you and it must be defined.

Many of us need to strengthen our belief in self. Affirmations are so important. These positive short messages, sentences and words are necessary to speak aloud daily to ourselves to communicate just how important and special we are. Journaling and affirmations helped me. I truly believe in them, and I know now that learning how to speak positive things about ourselves is how we can turn around the message that we have of ourselves and make something better. I tell myself I am fearfully and wonderfully made. I AM INTELLIGENT. I AM QUALIFIED. I AM AWESOME. I didn't tell myself those things before. I've learned so much in this process. That I control my destiny with God's help, by speaking and thinking positive about myself.

What I believe, in my opinion and I don't have the statistic on this, but I've found it to be true; but about 97% of abusers are cowards. They are looking for somebody that they can prey on, to take advantage of, because that person is weak. When we build ourselves up, then cowards who prey on weak people, can't take advantage of us. If I had believed in myself enough, I wouldn't have ended up in that relationship. It would have been very different. I either would not have been abused nor would I have been with an abuser to begin with. The thing that holds us all back is our silence. We need to talk about it. Give a voice to this silent epidemic.

Domestic violence has no face, no creed, no color, no age, none of that. Anybody and everybody could and should talk about it, but it is taboo. Nobody really wants to talk about it, because either they know somebody who is in an abusive relationship or they've been affected by abuse themselves. Or maybe they just feel that they should mind their own business. I've heard people say, "If they want to be in it, then that's on them." People don't choose to be in those types of relationships, sometimes they just end up there. Yes, there are signs and signals which we will talk about later. However, most abusers don't wear badges and ids. They don't walk up to the person they are interested in and say 'Hello, I'm an abuser. I'm insecure, manipulative and I have issues that will cause me to mistreat you, disrespect you and probably physically assault you. Would you like to go out with me and possible start a long and horrific relationship that's full of hurt and disappointment?' Instead, they are charismatic, they are charming, they are scheming and they are cunning to say the least. They catch people at their weakest moments to make them think that they are always going to be there, that they are the only ones who care about them and they are the only ones that are going to love them the way that they need to be loved. Does that sound familiar? Of course it does, every love story starts out that way, but some don't have happily ever after endings.

WHEN THEY ARE READY TO TALK

When talking to people that are in an abusive relationship if they are open to have the conversation, that means that they are looking for help. So strategically I let them know a couple of things:

1. I'm someone that they can confide in.
2. The best thing they can do is strategize for a safe departure from the relationship.
3. If they make a plan and follow the plan, then they too can live on this side of abuse.

Anyone trying to escape abuse has to be careful because abusers will try to woo them back and sometimes those people who go back, don't get another chance to get out again. One of the things about domestic violence is, statistics say that it takes a victim almost seven times before they actually come out of an abusive relationship. That's not everybody, but the majority. Sometimes those people in those seven times, because they go back and forth, back and forth, back and forth, they don't make it to the seventh time. Those are the ones that usually end in some type of violent death, or they end up killing their abuser and ending up in prison, because they didn't have a record of the abuse before. Or they may even take their own lives, suicide.

It is my job, my passion, and my calling to bring awareness to anybody and everybody and to make sure the victim knows that there are ways out. There are people out here that want to help them and they can get help, they have to have an open mind to the help make a conscious decision that this is something that they want.

That's why my non-profit, 4 MY VOICE MATTERS, NFP., raises awareness through conversations more than anything else. We raise funds to help people have a voice. To have those intimate conversations on the topics that are typically taboo. We want to give a safe place to share what they've been through, and know that they are safe, and that people understand.

As I mentioned before, abusers are charismatic, manipulative individuals that convince us that the abused are in the wrong. They insist that the victims are the ones that need help. But as we have open conversations, it helps us to be able to build ourselves up. To gain trust in ourselves. To come out from underneath of the shadow of that abuse and know that there is a safe space. I want to be here for you. To be somebody that you can confide in. To help you strategize a safe departure. To make a plan. To follow that plan and know that you can live on the other side of abuse. Yes, your abuser will try to woo you back. But when you have a strategy, you can succeed.

THERE IS A WAY OUT

Once you make the decision that leaving is something that you want to do, there is a way out. You can break the cycle of abuse. The first step is acknowledging that an abusive cycle exists in our lives. I've already shared how the cycle works, so if you recognize it and are ready to end it, CONGRATULATIONS. Even if you've been approached by someone who is ready to end the cycle and you are committed to help them, this is great. Step one is accomplished and now we can continue.

Even while we are in the cycle, we must begin making an exit strategy. This must be done strategically and wisely as not to agitate the abuser, and/or put ourselves and loved ones in danger. We have to listen to the conversations that are happening, and even more so be aware of the responses that are happening. It's called a honeymoon period because they are lavishing you with gifts, love and affection, kind words and they give you half an apology, but 9 times out of 10, at the end of the apology, it's a, "Well, if you wouldn't have done this..., I wouldn't have had to..." So I always tell people just be aware of the conversation. Be aware of how they are responding to you and how you respond to them. But also take mental note of how many times it's happening. How many times the cycle is repeating itself and is it happening more frequently now? I remember a time where the abuse started and then it stopped for maybe six or seven months, and I thought we were going to be ok, that he didn't need to get the help that I kept asking him to get, and that we were better. Then, either the world pissed him off or just my presence made him mad because that day he came home, he began yelling and screaming after I spoke to him. I don't remember what I said, but I remember the slap to the mouth. Then the abuse started again, and it became—more frequent. Abusers also tend to escalate after a season. Usually the abuse gets worse, it doesn't lighten up. So, I would always tell people during the honeymoon phase, just be aware and take note of exactly what the abuser doing. And how soon after the honeymoon phase are we right back into the cycle where the abuse starts again.

As we go through the cycle, we need to take a mental note of how many times it's happening. This may be a weird analogy to some, but it's like monitoring the contractions of an expecting mom. The more frequent and intense the contractions become, the closer they are to delivery. The more frequent and intense the abuse cycle phases become, the more likely this will irrupt into imminent and possible fatal danger. Is it happening more frequently? Is it getting worse? Also, we need to take note of how does he act, and what does he do during the honeymoon phase? And how soon will this "honeymoon phase" end and the abuse happen again?

I know some of you find yourself knowing that you've been abused, but you still believe so strongly in the possibility that this person you love and live with will change. I don't make excuses for my ex. What I do say is this, my ex-husband was somebody who was very charismatic, he was very kind and he was the life of the party. This man was caring by nature and would give you the shirt off his back. He just could not translate all that love and care into his intimate relationships or as a husband towards his wife. With that in mind when people defend their abusers, I believe them wholeheartedly. I believe that at some point in time, that the abuser had to be a good person for you to even want to be involved with them. I mean, who walks down the street and sees somebody jumping on somebody else or just being mean for no apparent reason and say, "Hey, you look like the type of person that I want to be in a relationship with! Leave the person you're jumping on, come be with me. I'm going to start dating you and we are going to make this work!" Nobody says that.

We often meet people who are charming, attractive, intelligent, and that attracts us in more ways than one. However, there is no manual that explains that time, circumstances, finance and the lack there of, and just pressures of life can change who we are and who we become. How individuals are raised, taught, and treated long before they meet you shape how they interact with you and vice versa. So, instead of placing blame, or judgement for people in abusive situations, you can do a few other things like: check yourself and your relationship for signs of abuse, be more vigilant and alert in case someone around you in your circle is indicating the need for help and educate yourself on how to help victims and survivors. We often meet the person that would like to be on our good side, that would like to lavish us with time, with compliments, saying that they want to be with us and only us. All this attention and being doted on makes you feel some kind of way. So, if you'll be honest with yourself, you want to spend time with them because this attention makes you feel good, special even. They have made themselves interesting and appealing to you. So, when people defend their abusers, I tell them, you either met a PR person for that individual and they deceived you from the beginning. Or you saw that rough, manipulative side of the individual and you decided to ignore it. Either way it goes, you are in it now and if you want to come out of it, you have to recognize those signs for what they are.

WE ALL SEE THE SIGNS

We all see the signs in our relationships.
During courtship, while living together early
on, or just in general things happen, incidents
occur and we ignore them for different
reasons. Maybe it's a strong desire to be with
that person, maybe we are attracted to the
lifestyle they can provide, maybe it's fear of
being alone for the rest of our lives, or may
we think we can change them? Whatever the
reason is, most of us have ignored signs at
one time or another in our lives. The only
difference is that the consequence of ignoring
signs, is more detrimental than others. Just
like street signs, we see street signs all the
time and if we ignore some of the street signs,

they either get us in trouble with the law or they can cause accidents, they can cause our demise. Whether we ignore them or follow them can dictate how our day is going to be. You look at stop signs, railroad crossing signs and one-way signs daily. You can relate the street signs to the abusive signs or red flags in your life. Prepare yourself. Be safe.

When I started talking to the youth about domestic violence, I picked street signs because I thought it would be something they could easily relate to. Then I realized that we all see and recognize street signs whenever we leave our homes. One of the street signs I use is "Stop". Red is an extreme color, but it's really funny how it can depict violence and it can also depict love and passion. So, I ask people, when you see a stop sign, you are supposed to stop, right? There is a reason that it's there, either the traffic going the other way doesn't have a stop sign, or they have a stop sign and you are supposed to give them the right of way or vice-versa. If not, there will be a collision in the intersection, which will cause pain, destruction, and sometimes even death. Red is such a vibrant color, it is there for a reason. And when we see it, we need to obey it. How many times do you perform what my dad calls a "California Stop"? Which is actually a rolling stop or treating a stop sign like a yield sign. Just pumping your brakes for a second, but you go through the stop because you are either in a hurry to get somewhere, you are late, or you just don't feel like stopping. Again, that stop sign is there for a reason and you should not ignore it because it's going to save your life or either stop you from going somewhere or doing something that's going to bring you harm. Same thing in a relationship. How many times have you had a feeling that you need to stop the relationship, stop entertaining being in a relationship with someone, because you see signs or possible signs that could be a problem in the future if you continue to pursue the relationship? Some stop signs even have flashing red lights with them to bring more attention to make you aware that this is a sign you should not ignore. Have you had red lights go off as bright as a siren is loud and you still chose or are choosing to ignore it?

Another one is, "One-Way." When they give you directions on streets, it's for a reason. I give downtown Chicago for an example. When you have a busy town, large city or metropolis usually they utilize one-way streets for a couple of reasons. It's because the area is so congested, to have two-way streets in the busiest parts of town are not feasible because the streets are not wide enough, or they are trying to control the flow of traffic to make sure everything runs more smoothly in these areas. Most one way streets are narrow. So narrow you can't park on both sides, you can only park on one side if parking is allowed at all. If you do park on both sides of the street, the actual driving lane is so narrow you could possibly hit a car on either side. But what would happen if you try to go down the wrong way on a one-way street? Here we go again, you are setting yourself up to possibly have a collision. You are setting yourself to get a ticketed by a cop. You are setting yourself up to possibly have someone come out of a car while you're going the wrong way and you can cause them harm or yourself. So, we are talking about direction. You always want to pay attention to what direction the relationship going? Do you see some signs that you should be paying close attention to? Does this relationship seem like it's one-sided or one dimensional, like the one-way street? That means that your partner is focused possibly on themselves, only themselves. They could care less about how you feel, what you feel, what you want or need, it's all about them. So, I suggest to people, watch out for the one sided, "one-way" person when you are in a relationship, they can be abusive as well. Maybe not physically, but emotionally and verbally.

SPEED BUMP

Speed bumps. Speed bumps and speed bump signs are yellow, yellow means caution. When we look at caution, you can think of a railroad crossings sign which can also yellow. You should always proceed with caution by looking both ways. But a speed bump, is placed where they are placed for a reason. Maybe it's down a residential street where kids play. You are only supposed to go 15 or 20 miles per hour, but people will always try to go 5 or 10 above the speed limit.

If you're like me I know you have a little lead in that driving foot, ha ha ha. That speed bump is there so that you know that you need to slow down. If you don't slow down, you may fly over the speed bump and you could possibly do damage to the underbody of your vehicle. If there are kids out there, you won't have time enough to stop after riding fast over a speed bump. You may hit a kid, you may hit a car, you may hit an adult, or you may lose control and hit a sturdy structure. When it comes to relationships, speed bumps are put in place to help us realize, understand and look at the relationship and say, "Ooh, I need to slow down." Maybe something is out of whack. Maybe that person is moving too fast. Maybe you're moving too fast. Are you in a rush to not be alone, in a rush to be married, in a rush to share your space? Are you rushing into this relationship not taking time to get to know your partner? SPEED BUMP! You may need to take a step back and SLOW DOWN.

One of the things about my relationship that I remember is when we first started dating, within a month, he was already calling me his fiancé, or he was calling me his wife and having me do things that a wife should help take care of. Like taking care of bills or making phone calls for him pertaining to his personal business. I would even use his last name on the telephone, even though it didn't legally belong to me. That should have been that neon sign that glows brighter than a regular lighted sign to me. The sign was saying, "Whoa, pump your breaks Rená!" It seemed cute then, because I was young. I would say to myself, "Oh, he called me his fiancé. Oh, I'm wifey." But if I look back now, that was a big red flag that I should have been able to see, I should have been able to see the speed bump that my car went flying over. So, I tell people, speed bumps mean slow down, so please... slow down, pause, take a step back and examine what you could possibly be getting yourself into.

The last sign is "Dead End". Dead end is self-explanatory. If you take yourself down a dead end street, you are going to get caught up. There is really no way out of it, unless you can back up. And 9 times out of 10, you will not be able to back up, because by the time you turn down the dead-end street, there could possibly be someone behind you, blocking you in. Worst case scenario is somebody blocking you in, if that person means you harm, that may be your demise. You can't turn down an alley. Alleys aren't commonly seen on a dead-end street. Imagine being stuck in a dead-end relationship. You are in a rut. You find yourself in this abusive relationship, where can you go? You could try to leave, but usually the person that is blocking you in is the person that is pretty much holding your fate in their hands, and you have to kind of judge by their temperature, how you should respond. If you saw a sign that says, "Dead End" and you don't live on that block, you have no business down that block, when you know that there is no way for you to turn around, there is no reason you should go down a dead-end street. If you see the signs that your partner is possibly abusive you shouldn't try to continue the relationship. One thing I do know is that abuse is a LEARNED behavior. An abuser has to want to be 'taught' how to 'unlearn' being abusive. Dead ends mean dead, stop, no more. It could be your demise in life, and that sign is also yellow. Yellow means communication as well as caution. We need to learn how to communicate more. Sometimes I think that when people show you themselves, we are afraid to ask the questions that we need to ask to see what type of response we are going to get. We need to see if they are going to typically be honest with us. You know, most people have an inner being or something that gives you a gut feeling when somebody is not telling you the truth. We just tend to ignore it. Or we tend to overlook it. Or we think, "Oh well that happened, and it wasn't that bad. Let's wait and see if something else happens." Those are the signs that we need to look for and choose not to ignore them.

I CAN'T SEE MY REFLECTION

I also talk about a concept called, "Vampire Syndrome" which is syndrome that cause us to symbolically look in the mirror of our own lives and literally see no reflection. It's kind of funny when I think about it. Growing up, I used to watch vampire movies all the time. I used to be very, very fascinated. Whether they were the scary movies or the ones where they made them comical. One of the things that I know about vampires, in the fiction part of it is, they cast no reflection. In casting no reflection, it's like when you are in an abusive relationship. You see everything going on around you. You can detect the signs of the cycle of abuse in everyone else's relationship. You can see their spouses using money as a punishment or controlling device. You notice concealer coverage for a light facial scar, or that they haven't been allowed to take call or come out of the house in a week or so. The tricky part about this "vampire syndrome" though is that you will be staring in the mirror, but you don't see your true reflection. It's like you are standing there looking at nothing, because you refuse to accept that you are in an abusive relationship. You refuse to accept that you don't have everything together. Most vampires, the reason why they became so attractive to me, is because I've never seen a vampire that didn't have everything together. They were charismatic. They were attractive. They walk with swag. They gave you the appearance that life was grand on their side. That if you came to their side, they would promise you eternity and the only thing you had to do is sleep during the day, stay away from garlic and holy water, but you could actually live. You would never get old. But in the interim, what everybody failed to realize is, you had to die in order to be grand. I equate the life of an 'undead' person to that of a person in a domestic violence relationship.

I believe for me, myself personally, that I lived a life of the walking dead for the longest. I became the fiction character that I admired so much. I put on airs to make others believe that I had it all together. Hoping that if they cared, they would believe that I was happy and living the best life with my husband and two dogs. That life was good in our home in the suburbs. I made it look on the outside to everyone else, that I was living a grand life. That I was happy. That everything was fine. That he was the best husband ever and that my life was just great. And it really wasn't. All fiction just like the vampire movies I enjoyed watching. I really wasn't alive when I was in my relationship. Why? Because I was living for him, and to please him. I was doing everything he wanted me to do, and no matter what I did, it was not pleasing to him. I was cut down so many times emotionally, verbally, physically, and financially. And every time I looked in the mirror, I saw my reflection fade away little by little, until I had no reflection. Why? Because I wasn't who I was before I started the relationship, I had agreed or accepted to live my life as a vampire, but hadn't realized it.

If you have recognized the signs and the cycles, and created a strategy to find a way out, there are people like myself that are here to help you. Again, I want you to hear me. I'm not saying that the person can't be great. But we do know that if they are abusing you, they aren't great for you. Your abuser may be the most wonderful person in the world, but they don't need to be in a relationship right now. They need help.

DESTINY DEFINED

What I came to understand is that although this happened to me, it wasn't about me. I believe if it was about me, I wouldn't be here to share what is on these pages with you. I could have been permanently paralyzed. I could have needed organs for transplants since my organs were hit by bullets. Or I would look like someone who has been shot, but I don't. God will define for you a destiny. He has always had it for you. Am I saying that God made this happen to you? Absolutely not! Keep in mind that all mankind has free will. What I am suggesting in this chapter is that from the beginning of time we are filled with purpose, gifts, and destiny. And, along our life's journey we have defining moments, experiences, and situations that mold and shape us to be more effective and impactful in whatever our purpose calls for from us. Do this for just a few moments. Think of all the successful people you like and love? Let as many as possible come to mind. Then ask yourself, do you know some of the defining moments and stories they have share about how they got there? Of course you do. No one gets to the mountain top, without, cuts, bruises, falls, and challenge. And when they are transparent about how they reached a marker of success, it includes pain, failure, disappointment, etc. Maybe they experienced bankruptcy, homelessness, rejection, or even divorce before they rediscovered love again. Way back in 2008, my destiny was defined for me. I just didn't know it yet. I know now that the non-profit that I'm running and all the things that I do to help abuse victims just like you or someone you know, is exactly what God designed for me. I know that He has a destiny for you as well. We have to start out somewhere. For me, when I woke up after the shooting. First, I simply focused on my breathing. I took some deep breaths with tears rolling down my face and back into my ears, at the thought that I was alive. I survived the shooting and the surgery. Of course once I woke up my family and friends took shifts coming in and out of my room to see the miracle of life for themselves. Once the visits slowed down, and I had more moments alone, I began to journal. And now I can see that what I journaled about almost 10 years ago is coming to fruition. I prayed, I asked God to lead me to where he wanted me to go. The dream I had of writing a book to bring awareness to people of this horrible 'disease', called Domestic Violence, to help them find a way out, you are reading that dream book right now. The fact that you are holding it or were able to download it means that you are seeing my prayers being answered and God's hands at work.

So what can you do to be aware of the situation? There are the signs I told you about, and just like when we are driving down the road, we can both pay attention to the signs on the side of the road and drive safely, or we can ignore the signs and find ourselves in situations we didn't have to be in. Either way, the signs are there.

We find ourselves when we are in an abusive relationship either coming to a place where we see what's going on and we make a different choice, we create a strategy and a plan to leave, or we end up dead at the end of that dead-end street. Abuse is an epidemic in our world. It's not just something that's happening only in the United States. Everywhere you go in the world, there are people with bad intentions, and if we are not aware of who we are, if we are not affirming ourselves, building ourselves up, seeking and living in our destiny, someone will find a way to hurt us. They will succeed. Yes, we can get restraining orders, but we all know that a restraining order is just a piece of paper. Familiarize yourself with local organizations that can help you or someone you know and meet in the time of crisis. When you hear or see something, SAY SOMETHING or DO SOMETHING. Someone's life can be saved when you take action. Even if you want to remain anonymous for safety reasons, you can still contact local authorities, in hope that they respond in time. Do your very best not to blame yourself or judge others that are being abused. Always remember the A's that drives me in this DV mission for life:

Action – We are called to put motion behind our talk. We have to make sure those we love are safe. Help them plan a way of escape.

Awareness – We are called to talk about this epidemic and make all of mankind aware that Domestic Violence will no longer be tolerated. Everyone has a right to live free of fear and be love unconditionally. Love shouldn't hurt.

Advocacy – locate resources and share with those who need assistance. Let them know that there are several agencies that provide shelter and counsel.

Amplify - (your voice) Start conversations. The main problem is that no one talks about it, if it isn't directly affecting them. Give them a voice, be their voice, because their voice does matter.

As we believe in ourselves, we say to ourselves that we are fearfully and wonderfully made. That we are unique, incredible, dynamic, powerful and important. WE'RE AWESOME! We begin to allow our destiny to be defined and revealed in our lives. I know now that my destiny is being birthed. I know that God is doing what He has always been doing from the beginning of time birthing my destiny. There is a destiny for you as well. The planned assassination will be avoided, and now is the time for your destiny to be defined!

VIN – Very Important Numbers

National Domestic Violence Hotline
1-800-799-SAFE (7233)

Alabama Coalition Against Domestic Violence

(334) 832-4842 Fax: (334) 832-4803
(800) 650-6522 Hotline

Alaska Network on Domestic and Sexual Violence

(907) 586-3650 Fax: (907) 463-4493

Arizona Coalition to End Sexual and Domestic Violence

(602) 279-2900 Fax: (844) 252-3094
(800) 782-6400 Nationwide

Arkansas Coalition Against Domestic Violence

(501) 907-5612 Fax: (501) 907-5618
(800) 269-4668 Nationwide

California Partnership to End Domestic Violence

(303) 831-9632 Fax: (303) 832-7067
(888) 778-7091

Colorado Coalition Against Domestic Violence

(303) 831-9632 Fax: (303) 832-7067
(888) 778-7091

Connecticut Coalition Against Domestic Violence

(860) 282-7899 Fax: (860) 282-7892
(888) 774-2900 In State DV Hotline

Delaware Coalition Against Domestic Violence

(302) 658-2958 Fax: (302) 658-5049
(800) 701-0456 Statewide

DC Coalition Against Domestic Violence

(202) 299-1181 Fax: (202) 299-1193

Florida Coalition Against Domestic Violence

(850) 425-2749 Fax: (850) 425-3091

(800) 500-1119 In State

Georgia Coalition Against Domestic Violence

(404) 209-0280 Fax: (404) 766-3800
(800) 334-2836 Crisis Line

Hawaii State Coalition Against Domestic Violence

(808) 832-9316 Fax: (808) 841-6028

Idaho Coalition Against Sexual and Domestic Violence

(208) 384-0419 Fax: (208) 331-0687
(888) 293-6118 Nationwide

Illinois Coalition Against Domestic Violence

(217) 789-2830 Fax: (217) 789-1939

Indiana Coalition Against Domestic Violence

(317) 917-3685 Fax: (317) 917-3695
(800) 332-7385 In State

Iowa Coalition Against Domestic Violence

(515) 244-8028 Fax: (515) 244-7417
(800) 942-0333 In State Hotline

Kansas Coalition Against Sexual and Domestic Violence

(785) 232-9784 Fax: (785) 266-1874

Kentucky Domestic Violence Association

(502) 209-5382 Phone Fax (502) 226-5382

Louisiana Coalition Against Domestic Violence

(225) 752-1296 Fax: (225) 751-8927

Maine Coalition To End Domestic Violence

(207) 430-8334 Fax: (207) 430-8348

Maryland Network Against Domestic Violence

(301) 429-3601 Fax: (301) 809-0422
(800) 634-3577 Nationwide

Jane Doe, Inc./Massachusetts Coalition Against Sexual
Assault and Domestic Violence

(617) 248-0922 Fax: (617) 248-0902

Michigan Coalition Against Domestic and Sexual Violence

(517) 347-7000 Phone/TTY Fax: (517) 248-0902

Minnesota Coalition For Battered Women

(651) 646-6177 Fax: (651) 646-1527
(651) 646-0994 Crisis Line
(800) 289-6177 Nationwide

Mississippi Coalition Against Domestic Violence

(601) 981-9196 Fax: (601) 981-2501
(800) 898-3234

Missouri Coalition Against Domestic and Sexual Violence

(573) 634-4161 Fax: (573) 636-3728

Montana Coalition Against Domestic & Sexual Violence

(406) 443-7794 Fax: (406) 443-7818
(888) 404-7794 Nationwide

Nebraska Domestic Violence Sexual Assault Coalition

(402) 476-6256 Fax: (402) 476-6806
(800) 876-6238 In State Hotline
(877) 215-0167 Spanish Hotline

Nevada Network Against Domestic Violence

(775) 828-1115 Fax: (775) 828-9911

New Hampshire Coalition Against Domestic and Sexual Violence

(603) 224-8893 Fax: (603) 228-6096

New Jersey Coalition for Battered Women

(609) 584-8107 Fax: (609) 584-9750
(800) 572-7233 In State

New Mexico Coalition Against Domestic Violence

(505) 246-9240 Fax: (505) 246-9434

New York State Coalition Against Domestic Violence

(518) 482-5464 Fax: (518) 482-3807
(800) 942-5465 English-In State
(800) 942-6908 Spanish-In State

North Carolina Coalition Against Domestic Violence

(919) 956-9124 Fax: (919) 682-1449
(888) 997-9124

North Dakota Council on Abused Women's Services

(701) 255-6240 Fax: (701) 255-1904
(888) 255-6240 Nationwide

Action Ohio Coalition For Battered Women

(614) 825-0551 Fax: (614) 825-0673
(888) 622-9315 In State

Ohio Domestic Violence Network

(614) 781-9651 Fax: (614) 781-9652

(800) 934-9840

Oklahoma Coalition Against Domestic Violence and Sexual Assault

(405) 524-0700 Fax: (405) 524-0711

Oregon Coalition Against Domestic and Sexual Violence

(503) 230-1951 Fax: (503) 230-1973
(877) 230-1951

Pennsylvania Coalition Against Domestic Violence

(717) 545-6400 Fax: (717) 545-9456
(800) 932-4632 Nationwide

The Office of Women Advocates

(787) 721-7676 Fax: (787) 725-9248

Rhode Island Coalition Against Domestic Violence

(401) 467-9940 Fax: (401) 467-9943
(800) 494-8100 In State

South Carolina Coalition Against Domestic Violence and
Sexual Assault

(803) 256-2900 Fax: (803) 256-1030
(800) 260-9293 Nationwide

South Dakota Coalition Against Domestic Violence & Sexual
Assault

(605) 945-0869 Fax: (605) 945-0870
(800) 572-9196 Nationwide

Tennessee Coalition Against Domestic and Sexual Violence

(615) 386-9406 Fax: (615) 383-2967
(800) 289-9018 In State

Texas Council On Family Violence

(512) 794-1133 Fax: (512) 794-1199

Utah Domestic Violence Coalition

(801) 521-5544 Fax: (801) 521-5548

Women's Coalition of St. Croix

(340) 773-9272 Fax: (340) 773-9062

Vermont Network Against Domestic Violence and Sexual
Assault

(802) 223-1302 Fax: (802) 223-6943
(802) 223-1115 TTY

Virginia Sexual & Domestic Violence Action Alliance

(804) 377-0335 Fax: (804) 377-0339

Washington State Coalition Against Domestic Violence

(360) 586-1022 Fax: (360) 586-1024

Washington State Native American Coalition Against
Domestic and Sexual Assault

(360) 352-3120 Fax: (360) 357-3858
(888) 352-3120

West Virginia Coalition Against Domestic Violence

(304) 965-3552 Fax: (304) 965-3572

End Domestic Abuse Wisconsin: The Wisconsin Coalition
Against Domestic Violence

(608) 255-0539 Fax: (608) 255-3560

Wyoming Coalition Against Domestic Violence and Sexual
Assault

(307) 755-5481 Fax: (307) 755-5482
(800) 990-3877 Nationwide

National Suicide Hotline

1-800-273-TALK (8255)

Bullying and other teen related issues are causing our youth to take their lives at an alarming rate. 4 My Voice Matters now has a branch that is dedicated to suicide awareness and prevention. T.A.B. (Talk About Bullying) was started to honor the memory of Trinity Ann Banks who left us far too soon due to being bullied and feeling that she wasn't good enough. It is our job to encourage our youth and to let them know that their lives and voice do matter. If you know of anyone contemplating suicide, please seek assistance immediately. Contact the National Suicide Hotline at the number listed above.

Made in the USA
Middletown, DE
21 January 2019